DYNAMIC
PROGRAMMING

For the

Day Before Your Coding Interview

DCI series

Aditya Chatterjee x Ue Kiao

With Dynamic Programming,

you can crush any search space in seconds

Aditya Chatterjee **x** Ue Kiao

BE A NATIONAL PROGRAMMER

INTRODUCTION

Dynamic Programming is a fundamental algorithmic technique which is behind solving some of the toughest computing problems.

In this book, we have covered some Dynamic Programming problems which will give you the general idea of formulating a Dynamic Programming solution and some practice on applying it on a variety of problems.

The first chapter is the Dynamic Programming cheatsheet. This is a **goldmine**. This will help you get the core DP idea of over 50 problems within 30 minutes. You should revisit and revise this cheatsheet every 2 months.

Some of the problems we have covered are:

- **Permutation coefficient**

This is a basic problem but is significant in understanding the idea behind Dynamic Programming. We have used this problem to:

- o Present the two core ideas of Dynamic Programming to make the idea clear and help you understand what Dynamic Programming mean.
- o Show another approach which has the same performance (in terms of time complexity) and understand how it is different from our Dynamic Programming approach

- **Longest Common Substring**

This is an important problem as we see how we can apply Dynamic Programming in string problems. In the process, we have demonstrated the core ideas of handling string data which helps in identifying the cases when Dynamic Programming is the most efficient approach.

- **XOR value**

This is another significant problem as we are applying Dynamic Programming on a Number Theory problem more specifically problem involving subset generation. The search space is exponential in size but with our efficient approach, we can search the entire data in polynomial time which is a significant improvement.

This brings up a fundamental power of Dynamic Programming: Search exponential search space in polynomial time

- **K edges**

In line with our previous problems, in this problem, we have applied Dynamic Programming in a graph-based problem. This is a core problem as in this we learn that:

  o Dynamic Programming makes the solution super-efficient
  o Extending the Dynamic Programming solution using Divide and Conquer enables us to solve it more efficiently

This problem shows a problem where Dynamic Programming is not the most efficient solution but is in the right path.

We have covered other relevant solutions and ideas as well so that you have the complete idea of the problems and understand deeply the significance of Dynamic Programming in respect to the problems.

Book: **Dynamic Programming for the day before your Coding Interview**

Authors (2): Aditya Chatterjee, Ue Kiao

About the authors:

Aditya Chatterjee is an Independent Researcher, Technical Author and the Founding Member of OPENGENUS, a scientific community focused on Computing Technology.

Ue Kiao is a Japanese Software Developer and has played key role in designing systems like TaoBao, AliPay and many more. She has completed her B. Sc in Mathematics and Computing Science at National Taiwan University and PhD at Tokyo Institute of Technology.

Published: April 2020 (Edition 1)

Latest update: 22 August 2024

Publisher: © OpenGenus

ISBN: 9798640923216

Contact: team@opengenus.org

Available on Amazon as E-Book and Paperback.

TABLE OF CONTENTS

Recommended Books

- <u>Linked List Problems</u>: For Interviews and Competitive Programming
- <u>Problems on Array</u>
- <u>Binary Tree Problems</u>
- <u>Dynamic Programming on Trees</u>

- <u>Day before Coding Interview</u> series
- <u>#7daysOfAlgo</u> series

CHEATSHEET: Dynamic Programming

This cheatsheet will be useful to recap all core concepts in solving over 50 important Dynamic Programming problems within an hour.

To get the best benefit out of this cheatsheet, **go through the other 4 chapters first** and get used to the idea of Dynamic Programming. **This cheatsheet should be revised every 2 months.**

Categories of Problems where Dynamic Programming is applicable are:

- Any problem where answers to smaller problem can be used to find the answer to larger problem
- Problems involving combinatorics and permutation
- Finding a subsequence, supersequence, subset with a property
- Generating a sequence
- Maximum/Minimum property in paths or sub-tree in Tree data structures

- **Longest Increasing Subsequence**

```
dp[i] = Length of Longest Increasing subsequence where the last element
        is the ith element A[i]
```

The base case is:

```
dp[i] = 1 (by default)
```

The recursive relation is:

```
dp[i] = 1 + maximum(dp[j])
        where 0 < j < i AND a[j] <= a[i]
```

The answer is the maximum value in the DP array.

Approach	Time Complexity	Space Complexity
Brute Force	$O(2^N \times N)$	$O(1)$
Dynamic Programming	$O(N^2)$	$O(N)$

Longest Common Increasing Subsequence

Let the two arrays be arr1 and arr2.

The Dynamic Programming structure is as follows:

```
dp[j] = length of Longest common increasing
        subsequence ending with arr2[j]
```

The recursive relation is:

```
# If a common element is found in both arrays
if arr1[i] == arr2[j]:
    dp[j] = max(current+1, dp[j])


# If arr1 element is greater, current variable is updated
if arr1[i] > arr2[j]:
    current = max(current, dp[j])
```

Approach	Time Complexity	Space Complexity
Brute Force	$O(2^N \times (N+M))$	$O(1)$
Dynamic Programming	$O(N \times M)$	$O(M)$

Longest Increasing Odd Even Subsequence

```
dp[j] = length of Longest increasing odd
        even subsequence ending with arr[j]
```

The recursive relation is:

```
if (arr[i] > arr[j]
    and (arr[i]+arr[j]) % 2 != 0
    and dp[i] < dp[j] + 1)
        dp[i] = dp[j] + 1
```

Approach	Time Complexity	Space Complexity
Brute Force	$O(2^N \times (N))$	$O(1)$
Dynamic Programming	$O(N^2)$	$O(N)$

Shortest Common SuperSequence

Given two strings X and Y, the supersequence of string X and Y is such a string Z that both X and Y is subsequence of Z.

```
dp[i][j] = length of shortest common
           supersequence of First i characters
           of string S1 and First j characters
```

of string S2

Base cases:

```
dp[i][j] = j        if i == 0
dp[i][j] = i        if j == 0
```

The relation is:

```
dp[i][j] = dp[i - 1][j - 1] + 1
           if S1[i] == S2[j]
```

else

```
dp[i][j] = 1 + MINIMUM(dp[i - 1][j],
             dp[i][j - 1])
```

Approach	Time Complexity	Space Complexity
Brute Force	$O(N^N)$	$O(1)$
Dynamic Programming	$O(N^2)$	$O(N^2)$

Maximum Sum Subsequence

```
dp[i] = Sum of maximum sum subset with ith
        element as the last element of the
        subset
```

This recursive relation is captured by the following relation:

```
dp[i] = 1 + dp[i - 1]    ……  if dp[i] >= 0
      = dp[i - 1]        ……  if dp[i] < 0
```

Approach	Time Complexity	Space Complexity
Brute Force	$O(N \times 2^N)$	$O(1)$
Greedy Algorithm	$O(N)$	$O(1)$
Dynamic Programming	$O(N)$	$O(N)$

Maximum Sum Subsequence of size K

```
dp[i][j] = Sum of Largest sum subset with first i elements and length j
           with the jth element as the last element in the subsequence
```

Base cases:

```
dp[i][0] = 0    ……    for all i from 0 to N
dp[0][j] = 0    ……    for all j from 0 to N
dp[i][1] = A[i] ……    for all i fron 0 to N
```

Relation:

```
// Compute the relation
for i from 1 to N
    for j from 0 to i-1
        for m from 1 to K (size)
            dp[i][l + 1] = MAXIMUM(dp[i][l + 1],
                           dp[j][l] + A[i])
```

Approach	Time Complexity	Space Complexity
Brute Force	$O(N \times 2^N)$	$O(1)$
Dynamic Programming	$O(N^2)$	$O(N^2)$

Maximum Sum Increasing Subsequence

```
dp[i] = Sum of Longest Increasing subset with
        ith element as the last element of the
        subset
```

Base case:

```
for i from 0 to N
    dp[i] = A[i] // i-th element
```

The recursive relation is as follows:

```
// Compute the recursive relation
for i from 1 to N
    for j from 0 to i-1
        if A[i] > A[j]
            if dp[i] < dp[j] + A[i]
                dp[i] = dp[j] + A[i];
```

Approach	Time Complexity	Space Complexity
Brute Force	$O(N \times 2^N)$	$O(1)$
Dynamic Programming	$O(N^2)$	$O(N)$

Maximum Sum Increasing Subsequence of size K

```
dp[i][j] = Sum of Longest sum subset with first
           i elements and length j with the jth
           element as the last element in the
           subsequence
```

Base cases:

```
dp[i][0] = 0    ......   for all i from 0 to N
dp[0][j] = 0    ......   for all j from 0 to N
dp[i][1] = A[i] ......   for all i fron 0 to N
```

Relation:

```
for i from 1 to N
    for j from 0 to i-1
        if (A[j] < A[i])
            for m from 1 to K (size)
                dp[i][l + 1] = MAXIMUM(dp[i][l + 1],
                                    dp[j][l] + A[i])
```

Approach	Time Complexity	Space Complexity
Brute Force	$O(N \times 2^N)$	$O(1)$
Dynamic Programming	$O(N^2)$	$O(N^2)$

Variants of last 4 problems:

Number	Approach	Time Complexity	Space Complexity
1	Maximum Sum	$O(N)$	$O(N)$
2	#1 + size K	$O(N^2)$	$O(N^2)$
3	#1 + Increasing order	$O(N^2)$	$O(N)$
4	#3 + size K	$O(N^2)$	$O(N^2)$

Maximum Sum Alternating Subsequence

```
increase[i] = Sum of Maximum sum Alternating subsequence with A[i] being the
              last element and is greater than the previous element
```

```
decrease[i] = Sum of Maximum sum Alternating subsequence with A[i] being the
              last element and is less than the previous element
```

The base case is as follows:

```
increase[0] = A[0]

decrease[0] = A[0]
```

This results in:

```
increase[i] = Maximum(decrease[j] + A[i])

            …… for all j < i and A[i] > A[j]
```

```
decrease[i] = Maximum(increase[j] + A[i])

          ...... for all j < i and A[i] < A[j]
```

```
Answer = Maximum(increase[i], decrease[i])
          ......   for all i
```

Approach	Time Complexity	Space Complexity
Brute Force	$O(N \times 2^N)$	$O(1)$
Dynamic Programming	$O(N^2)$	$O(N)$

Longest Alternating Subsequence

If a sequence $\{a_1, a_2, ..., a_N\}$ is in alternating order, then:

- $a_1 > a_2$
- $a_i > a_{i+1}$ if i is odd and i != 1
- $a_i < a_{i+1}$ if i is even

```
increase[i] = Length of the longest Alternating subsequence with A[i]
            being the last element and is greater than the previous element
```

```
decrease[i] = Length of the longest Alternating subsequence with A[i]
            being the last element and is less than the previous element
```

The base case is as follows:

```
increase[0] = 1; Considering: A[0]

decrease[0] = 1; Considering: A[0]
```

This results in:

```
increase[i] = Maximum(decrease[j] + 1)
              // 1 for A[i]

              ...... for all j < i and A[i] > A[j]
```

```
decrease[i] = Maximum(increase[j] + 1)
              // 1 for A[i]

              ...... for all j < i and A[i] < A[j]
```

```
Answer = Maximum(increase[i], decrease[i])
         ......   for all i
```

Approach	Time Complexity	Space Complexity
Brute Force	$O(N \times 2^N)$	$O(1)$
Dynamic Programming	$O(N^2)$	$O(N)$

Newman Conway Sequence

Newman Conway sequence follows the following Recurrence Relation:

```
P(n) = P(P(n - 1)) + P(n - P(n - 1))
where,
P(n) = n-th number in Newman Conway Sequence
with P(1) = P(2) = 1
```

The basic idea is as follows:

```
int ncs[n + 1];
// Base case
ncs[0] = 0;
ncs[1] = 1;
```

```
ncs[2] = 1;
// Bottom-up dynamic programming approach
for (int i = 3; i <= n; i++)
    ncs[i] = ncs[ncs[i - 1]] + ncs[i - ncs[i - 1]];
```

Longest Arithmetic Progression

```
DP[i][diff] = Longest Arithmetic Subsequence with last element as
arr[i] and the difference being diff
// Base case:
All DP[i][diff] = 0
longest = 2
// Relation:
// For all pairs of (arr[j], arr[i]), diff = arr[i] - arr[j]
// Last 2 elements are arr[j] and arr[i]
DP[i][diff] = DP[j][diff] + 1      if DP[j][diff] > 0
              2                    otherwise
longest = max(longest, DP[i][diff]);
```

Approach	Time Complexity	Space Complexity
Brute Force	$O(N \times 2^N)$	$O(1)$
Dynamic Programming	$O(N^2)$	$O(N^2)$

Number of arithmetic progression subsequences

```
DP[i][diff] = Number of AP series with last element as arr[i] and
difference as diff
SUM[i][diff] = Sum of DP[j][diff] where arr[j] = i

// Base case
All DP[i][diff] = 1
diff range from (MIN - MAX) to (MAX - MIN)
ANSWER = 0

// Relation
For all diff:
DP[i][diff] += SUM[arr[i] - diff]     if arr[i] - diff >= 1
```

```
ANSWER += DP[i][diff] - 1;
SUM[a[i]][diff] += DP[i][diff];
```

Approach	Time Complexity	Space Complexity
Brute Force	$O(N \times 2^N)$	$O(1)$
Dynamic Programming	$O(N * MAX)$	$O(N * MAX)$

Longest Bitonic Subsequence

A bitonic sequence is a sequence which is first increasing to a peak value and then decreasing that is it is of the following form:

```
x1, x2, x3, ... xn
where:
    x1 < x2 < x3 < ... < xm
    xm > xm+1 > xm+2 > ... > xn
```

```
LIS[i]: length of the Longest Increasing subsequence ending at arr[i]
LDS[i]:  length of the longest Decreasing subsequence starting from arr[i]

LIS[0] = {1}
LIS[i] = {Max(LIS[j])} + 1 where j < i and arr[j] < arr[i]
       = arr[i], if there is no such j

LDS[n] = {1}
LDS[i] = 1+ {Max(LDS[j])} where j > i and arr[j] < arr[i]
       = arr[i], if there is no such j

LIS[i]+LDS[i]-1: the length Longest Bitonic Subsequence with peak at i
We need to find the position i with maximum value of LIS[i]+LDS[i]-1
```

Approach	Time Complexity	Space Complexity
Brute Force	$O(N \times 2^N)$	$O(1)$

Dynamic Programming	$O(N^2)$	$O(N^2)$

Maximum Sum Bitonic Subsequence

We have to maintain two arrays namely:

- MSB[i] indicates the maximum sum of increasing bitonic subsequence ending at element A[i]
- MSD[i] indicates the sum of decreasing bitonic subsequence starting at A[i].

```
Maximum sum bitonic subsequence = MAX(MSB[i] + MSD[i] - Arr[i])
```

Initialize MSB and MSD with the initial values:

```
for (int i = 0; i < n; i++)
{
    MSB[i] = arr[i];
    MSD[i] = arr[i];
}
```

Calculate MSB values:

```
// Compute MSB values from left to right
for (int i = 1; i < n; i++)
{
    for (int j = 0; j < i; j++)
    {

            if (arr[i] > arr[j] && MSB[i] < MSB[j] + arr[i])

            MSB[i] = MSB[j] + arr[i];

    }
}
```

Calculate MSD values:

```
// Compute MSD values from right to left
```

```
for (int i = n - 2; i >= 0; i--)
{
    for (int j = n - 1; j > i; j--)
    {
        if (arr[i] > arr[j] && MSD[i] < MSD[j] + arr[i])
        MSD[i] = MSD[j] + arr[i];
    }
}
```

Calculate the final maximum value using MSB and MSD:

```
// Find the maximum value of MSB[i] + MSD[i] - arr[i]
for (int i = 0; i < n; i++)
{
    max = max(max, (MSD[i] + MSB[i] - arr[i]));
}
```

Approach	Time Complexity	Space Complexity
Brute Force	$O(N \times 2^N)$	$O(1)$
Dynamic Programming	$O(N^2)$	$O(N)$

Find if a Subset with sum divisible by m exist

```
DP[i] = true if subset with sum S modulo m = i exists
```

```
if DP[j] == true and for each arr[i]
    set DP[ (j+arr[i])%m ] = true
    set temp[ (j+arr[i])%m ] = true
```

```
if temp[i] = true
```

```
    set DP[i] = true
```

```
DP[0] is our answer
```

Approach	Time Complexity	Space Complexity
Brute Force	$O(N^2)$	$O(1)$
Dynamic Programming	$O(N\,M)$	$O(N)$

Longest Geometric Progression

The structure of Dynamic Programming will be:

```
DP[i][j] = LGP with the first element
           being array[i] and ratio being j
```

If there are two elements array[i] and array[j] with ratio R and there is no common ratio as compared to previous element pairs, then:

```
DP[i][R] = 1
```

Else if there is common ratio R among previous elements, then:

```
DP[i][r] = DP[j][r] + 1
```

Answer is the maximum value in the matrix DP[][].

Kadane's algorithm for 1D

Solve problems like Maximum profit by buying and selling stock once.

arr[i] = price of stock on i^{th} day

-2	-3	4	-1	-2	1	5	-3

$$4 + (-1) + (-2) + 1 + 5 = 7$$

```
1. Initialize max_so_far = 0, max_ending_here = 0
2. Loop for each element of the array
   a) max_ending_here += a[i]
   b) if (max_ending_here < 0)
         max_ending_here = 0
      if (max_so_far <  max_ending_here)
         max_so_far = max_ending_here
3. return max_so_far
```

Time Complexity: O(N)

Space Complexity: O(1)

Maximum Sum Rectangle in a Matrix / 2D Kadane algorithm

1	2	-1	-4	-20
-8	-3	4	2	1
3	8	10	1	3
-4	-1	1	7	-6

Compress rows into a single value (sum) for all possible left and right column. This creates a 1D array. Apply 1D Kadane on this.

```
// Structure
maxSum = INT_MIN
temp[i] = sum between current left and right column for i-th row

// All possible left and right
```

```
// Create temp[i] = sum between current left and right column for i-th
row
// 1D array temp[] is created
// Apply 1D Kadane algorithm on temp[] = sum, start_index, end_index

for (int left = 0; left < col; left++)
{
    // Base case
    temp[i] = 0
    for (int right = left; right < col; right++)
    {
        for (i = 0; i < row; i++)
            temp[i] += arr[i][right];

        // Apply 1D Kadane algorithm
        // sum is sum of rectangle between (top, left) and (bottom,
right)

        int sum, top, bottom = kadane(temp);

        // Check maximum
        if (sum > maxSum)
        {
            maxSum = sum;
        }
    }
}

ANSWER = maxSum;
```

Approach	Time Complexity	Space Complexity
Brute Force	$O(N^5)$	$O(1)$
Dynamic Programming	$O(N^3)$	$O(N)$

Height of every node of Binary Tree

```
DP(X) = Height of node X


Base case:
DP(X) = -1 ; for every node X
```

```
The recursive relation is as follows:
DP(X) = MAXIMUM( DP(X.left) + DP(X.right)) + 1
```

Approach	Time Complexity	Space Complexity
Dynamic Programming	O(N)	O(N)

Diameter of Binary Tree using height of every node

```
height(X) = Height of node X
diameter = 0
```

If we are at a given node X and we know that the diameter passes through this node X, then there are 2 possibilities:

- Case 1: Diameter passes through the left and right child of node X
- Case 2: Diameter passes through only one child of node X. In this case, diameter goes to the parent of node X.

For Case 1, we have:

```
diameter = height(Left child of X) + height(Right child of X) + 1
```

Note, the diameter is the height of left child + height of right child + 1 (for node X).

Case 2:

In this case, diameter passes through only one child of node X. In this case, diameter goes to the parent of node X.

```
Diameter = Maximum(diameter of sub-tree at left child, diameter of sub
-tree at right child) + 1
```

Approach	Time Complexity	Space Complexity
Dynamic Programming	O(V+E)	O(V)

Largest Independent Set in Binary Tree

```
LISS(X) = largest independent set with node X as root
```

The recursive structure is as follows:

```
LISS(X) = MAX{ (1 + sum of LISS for all grandchildren of X), (sum of L
ISS for all children of X) }
```

The idea is simple, there are two possibilities for every node X:

- either X is a member of the set
- X is not a member.

The implications are:

- If X is a member, then the value of LISS(X) is 1 plus LISS of all grandchildren.
- If X is not a member, then the value is sum of LISS of all children.

Augment the tree to solve this efficiently. Augmented tree contains nodes having:

- data
- left child
- right child

- liss (an extra field)

The basic idea is as follows:

- the size of largest independent set excluding root is the size for the left tree + right tree. This is because at this point it might not be clear that including root is compatible or not.

```
size excluding root = size(root->left) + size(root->right)
```

- If we include the root, the minimum size is 1 and include the size of left node's children and right node's children. This is because left and right nodes cannot be included.

```
size including root = 1 + size(root->left->left) + size(root->left->right) + size(root->right->left) + size(root->right->right)
```

Approach	Time Complexity	Space Complexity
Dynamic Programming	O(V)	O(V)

Binary Lifting with kth ancestor

Binary Lifting is a technique used to find the kth ancestor of any node in a tree in $O(\log_2 N)$ time. This also leads to a faster algorithm in finding the lowest common ancestor (LCA) between two nodes in a tree.

The technique requires preprocessing the tree in O(N log N) using dynamic programming.

Structure:

```
DP[i][j] = 2^j -th ancestor of node i
```

The first step is to find out the 2j ancestor of every node where 0 <= j <= log(n). This can be done by dynamic programming.

The recursive relation is:

```
dp[i][j] = dp [dp[i][j-1]] [j-1]

where:
dp[i][j] = 2^j ancestor of i
dp[i][j-1] = 2^(j-1) ancestor of i
```

The expression essentially breaks down the path between a node and its ancestor into two parts. The following figure illustrates this relation

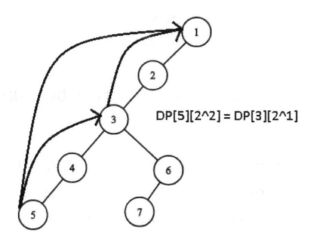

DP[5][2^2] = DP[3][2^1]

Note here that the fourth ancestor of Node 5 is the same as the second ancestor of Node 3.

The base case of the DP structure is:

1st ancestor = Parent of node

```
dp[i][j] = -1 for each pair i and j

dp[i][0] = 2⁰th ancestor of i = 1st ancestor of i=parent of i= parent[i]
```

Recursive relation:

```
for h = 1 to logN
    for i = 1 to N
        If dp[i][h-1] not equal to -1
            dp[i][h] = dp[dp[i][h-1]][h-1]
```

The kth ancestor can be calculated as follows:

- Decrease K by subtracting powers of two (say 2^h)
- Traverse to 2^h ancestor by using our DP structure

The LCA (Lowest Common Ancestor) between two nodes can be found as follows:

- Find the node at the lowest level (let us say a, otherwise swap them)
- Find the ancestor of a at the same level as b (let us call this node c).
- Find the lowest ancestors of b and c which are not equal.
- Return the parent of one of the nodes found in step 3.

```
// LCA of node a and b
If level[a] < level[b]
    swap a and b
```

```
c = a

// Find the ancestor of a at the same level of b
for i = logN to 0
    If level[c] - 2^i >= level[b]
        c = dp[c][i]

If b is equal to c
    return b

for i = logN to 0
    If dp[b][i] != -1 and dp[b][i] != dp[c][i]
        b = dp[b][i]
        c = dp[c][i]

return parent[b]
```

Complexity	Preprocessing of DP structure	Find kth ancestor	LCA
Best Case Complexity	O(N log N)	O(logN)	O(logN)
Average Case Complexity	O(N log N)	O(logN)	O(logN)
Worst Case Complexity	O(N log N)	O(logN)	O(logN)
Space Complexity	O(N log N)	O(1)	O(1)

Problem 1: Permutation coefficient

This is a simple problem but with this, we demonstrate the basic ideas of Dynamic Programming. This will enable you to formulate problems accordingly and apply Dynamic Programming.

The problem at hand is to compute a mathematical term known as "permutation coefficient".

What is Permutation Coefficient?

Permutation refers to the process of arranging all members of a given set to form a sequence. In case of permutation, order of elements is also considered.

To understand the permutation, let us take an example: Examine all the different ways in which a pair of objects can be selected from five distinguishable objects - A, B, C, D, E. If both the letters selected and order of selection are considered, then the following 20 outcomes are considered:

```
AB  BA  AC  CA  AD
DA  AE  EA  BC  CB
BD  DB  BE  EB  CD
DC  CE  EC  DE  ED
```

Each of these 20 possible selections is called a permutation. They can be called as permutations of five objects taken two at a time.

The number of permutations on a set of n elements is given by n!

Here, N! = N * (N-1) * (N-2) * ... * 1

The permutation coefficient is represented by P(N, K). It is used to represent the **number of ways to obtain an ordered subset of k elements from a set of N elements**.

```
P(N, K) = N! / (N-K)!

P(N, K) = number of ways of select K elements
          from N elements
```

Now, for a given value of N and K, we can compute the corresponding permutation coefficient P(N, K) as given by the equation.

The pseudocode of computing it will be as follows:

```
N, K (given)

answer = 1
for i from 1 to N
    answer = answer * i
for i from 1 to N-K
    answer = answer / i
```

```
answer (is our output)
```

There are some drawbacks of this approach:

- The answer can **overflow** as we are, first, calculating N! which is significantly larger than the answer
- If we calculate the coefficient for another value of N and K, we can reuse the value to compute another coefficient.

The first point of overflow can be tackled by observing the we can avoid the division and do multiplication only for required terms. The modified equation will be as follows:

```
P(N, K) = N! / (N-K)!

P(N, K) = (N-K+1) x (N-K+2) x ... x N
```

The pseudocode base on the above equation will be as follows:

```
N, K (given)

answer = 1
for i from N-K+1 to N
    answer = answer * i

answer (is our output)
```

The above approaches have a time complexity of O(N) to compute a given coefficient. Additionally, on computing a given coefficient, we cannot use it to compute another coefficient. There is no reuse.

Moreover, if we have to compute $O(N^2)$ coefficients, this approach will take **$O(N^3)$ time**. $O(N^2)$ coefficients is the number of coefficient P(i, j) where both i and j are less than equal to N.

We can optimized this by computing the factorials beforehand so that calculating each coefficient take constant time O(1) provided multiplication and division takes constant time.

In reality, multiplication and division has a minimum time complexity of **O(N log N)** for 2 N digit numbers.

The pseudocode if we precompute the factorial and use it to compute all coefficients will be as follows:

```
factorial[N+1]

// Precompute factorial
factorial[0] = 1
for i from 1 to N
    factorial[i] = factorial[i-1] * i

N, K (given)
```

```
answer = factorial[N] / factorial[N-K]
```

We can completely avoid the factorial as well if we compute factorial is reverse order that is:

Factorial(i) = i * (i+1) * ... * N

In this case, the answer of P(N, K) will be factorial(N-K+1).

The pseudocode of the above approach will be as follows:

```
factorial[N+1]

// Precompute factorial
factorial[N] = N
for i from N-1 to 0
    factorial[i] = factorial[i+1] * i

N, K (given)

answer = factorial[N-K+1]
```

With this solution, we can compute the value of N2 coefficients in O(N2) time with each coefficient taking constant time O(1).

Still, in this approach, the key is to precompute the factorial values and use them.

The problem of reusing the value of another coefficient is still open.

This is the starting part of solving this problem using Dynamic Programming.

We need to find a recursive relation in the original equation of Permutation coefficient. Let us go through the original equation once.

```
P(N, K) = N!/(N-K)!
```

If we consider a previous value say P(N-1, K), we see it as follows:

```
P(N-1, K) = (N-1)!/(N-K-1)!
```

One recursive relation, we get at this point is:

```
P(N, K) = P(N-1, K) * N / (N-K)
```

We are reusing previous value. As our goal is to generate all possible permutation coefficients, we need a variant of this recursive relation where:

- We will be able to capture other coefficients like P(N, K-1)
- We can avoid division as it is an expensive computing operation

The recursive relation that satisfies our requirements is as follows:

$$P(N, K) = P(N-1, K) + K * P(N-1, K-1)$$

In fact, there are several such recursive relation and you need to formulate one that fits the problem perfectly.

Hence, the **first step of solving a problem using Dynamic Programming** is to:

Formulate a relation to use the answer of a smaller problems (maybe multiple problems) to compute the answer of the larger problem

The recursive relation can be implemented recursively but it brings new problems. Let us see the pseudocode of the recursive approach:

```
int permutationCoeff(int n,int k)
{
    if(k == 0) return 1;
```

```
    if(k > n) return 0;
    return (k*permutationCoeff(n-1,k-1)+permutationCoeff(n-
1,k));
}
```

The problem with this is that each coefficient is computed multiple times, and this brings the time complexity to $O(2^N)$ that is exponential.

This is evident based on this image denoting recursive calls:

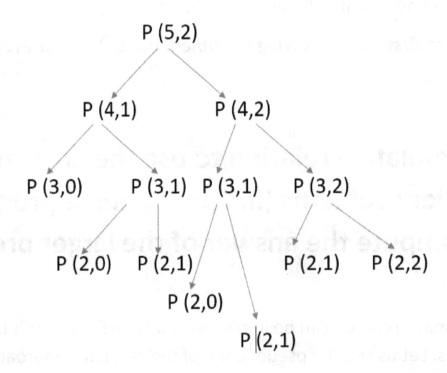

The idea of implementing this efficiently is that second step of Dynamic Programming. The idea is:

Store the value of each coefficient so that if it need not be computed again when the value is needed

To store previous values, we need to define a 2D array as follows:

DP[i][j] = Permutation coefficient P(i, j)

The recursive relation based on it is as follows:

```
DP[N][K] = DP[N-1][K] + K * DP[N-1][K-1]
```

The pseudocode will be as follows:

```
N, K (given)

P[N+1][K+1];
for i from 0 to N
     for j from 0 to MINIMUM(i, K)
    if(j==0)
      P[i][j] = 1;
         else
              P[i][j] = P[i-1][j] + j * P[i-1][j-1];
         P[i][j+1]=0;
```

Note that if K = O(N), then the time complexity of our Dynamic Programming approach will be $O(N^2)$. This is same as our approach of using precomputed factorial value.

The advantages we have in our Dynamic Programming approach is that:

- We are using precomputed values to generate new values
- There will be no overflow from cases where we generate numbers greater than the answer
- The multiplication involves smaller number and hence, is **faster in practice** but same in terms of time complexity.

A key idea is that even though time complexity remains same, different approaches will have different performance in real systems.

Think of this simple problem deeply and try to formulate other recursive relations and form Dynamic Programming solutions out of it.

Problem 2: Longest Common Substring

String problems are fundamental as it has properties distinct from numeric data. A common approach is to convert string to corresponding numeric data and work on it accordingly. In some problems, working on string data directly turns out to be efficient. We will explore **this idea of working on string data directly**.

This is an **important problem** as we will see how a simple approach (involving string manipulation ideas) has the same time complexity as the Dynamic Programming approach but in practice, Dynamic Programming approach is much faster.

Let us understand our current problem.

A substring is a contiguous sequence of characters within a string. For example, open is a substring of opengenus. Given two strings say S1 and S2, we need to find a string S3 which is a substring to both S1 and S2. We need to find the longest such string S3.

Let us understand this problem with examples.

Examples:

- S1 = opengenus

- S2 = genius
- S3 = gen

The longest common substring of str1(opengenus) and str2(genius) is "gen" of length 3. Other common substrings are "us", "g", "ge", "en" and much more.

"gen" is the longest such substring and hence, "gen" is the answer.

- S1 = carpenter
- S2 = sharpener
- S3 = arpen

The longest common substring of str1(carpenter) and str2(sharpener) is "arpen" of length 5.

Pause and think for a couple of minutes before proceeding further

---

Following is the summary of the approaches we will take one by one:

- Brute force **O(N⁴) time, O(1) space**
- Hashing approach **O(N²) time, O(N²) space**
- Dynamic Programming **O(N²) time, O(N) space**

The brute force approach to solve this is to generate all substrings of the first string S1 and for each substring, we need to check if it is a substring of the second string S2 as well. This way we need to maintain the length of the longest substring.

Steps:

- Set largest to 0
- For each substring A1 of string S1
    - Check if A1 is a substring of string S2 by comparing with all substrings of S2 of length L (length of substring A1)
    - If yes, check if its length is > largest, then set largest to length

This process takes $O(N^4)$ time for strings of length N as:

- There are $O(N^2)$ substrings of a string of length N
- There are $O(N)$ substrings of a given length L
- It takes $O(N)$ time to compare two strings of length N

Pseudocode:

```
S1 = string of length N
S2 = string of length M

for i from 0 to N
   for j from i to N
      substring = substring in S1 from i to j
      for k from 0 to M-(j-i+1)
         check = 1
         for l from k to k+(j-i+1)
            if S1.char(l) != S1.char(i+l-k)
               check = 0
               break
```

```
        if (check == 1 and result < (j-i+1))
            result = j-i+1

result is our answer
```

We can improve this brute force by the simple idea that:

"Strings can be transformed to Numeric data"

This will result in comparing strings in constant time O(1) instead of O(N) linear time.

The key idea of this approach is to convert strings to an integer using String hashing techniques so that the comparison time reduces to constant time O(1). This will bring the overall time complexity to O(N2).

Steps:

- For each substring of S1, generate hash and store it in a hashmap
- For each substring of S2, check if it exists in the hashmap and keep track of the longest substring.

Note that generating hash of a string of length N takes O(N) time. In this view, the overall time complexity stays $O(N^3)$ as there are $O(N^2)$ substrings.

This can be overcome as we can use the rolling hash technique to compute the hashing. The key idea is to use the hash of the previous substring to generate the hash of the next substring where only constant number of characters change. This results in O(N) time complexity for N strings that is constant average time O(1).

Steps:

- For each substring of S1, generate hash and store it in a hashmap using rolling hash technique
- For each substring of S2, check if it exists in the hashmap and keep track of the longest substring.

This brings the **time complexity to O(N^2)**.

We covered this point along with concepts like rolling hash in detail in the 4th problem in our book:

Problems for the day before your coding interview by Aditya Chatterjee & Ue Kiao (OpenGenus).

Problems for the day before your coding interview

By Aditya Chatterjee & Ue Kiao

OpenGenus.org

Find it on Amazon: **daybefore1.opengenus.org**

We will solve this problem using a Dynamic Programming approach. The time complexity will be same as our previous approach but in practice, this **Dynamic Programming approach** is much faster as it minimizes several operations.

This will be faster as it has less memory requirements than our previous hashing approach. The space complexity of **hashing approach** is $O(N^2)$ while our **Dynamic Programming** has space complexity as $O(2 \times N) = O(N)$.

Let the first string be s1 and second be s2. Suppose we are at DP state when the length of s1 is i and length of s2 is j, the result of which is stored in dp[i][j]. So, it means:

```
dp[i][j] = length of the longest substring in first i
           characters of S1 and first j characters of S2
```

Now if s1[i-1] == s2[j-1], then dp[i][j] = 1 + dp[i-1][j-1],

The recursive relation to compute the elements of the above DP array is as follows:

If the character at i[th] position of S1 is same as j[th] character of S2, then the longest substring considering first i characters of S1 and j characters of S2 is same as 1 + longest substring considering first i characters of S1 and j characters of S2.

Think of this carefully.

Following is the relation:

```
dp[i][j] = 1 + dp[i-1][j-1]   if s1[i-1] == s2[j-1]
```

To print the longest common substring, we use variable end. When dp[i][j] is calculated, it is compared with res where res is the maximum length of the common substring.

If res is less than dp[i][j], then end is updated to i-1 to show that longest common substring ends at index i-1 in s1 and res is updated to dp[i][j].

The longest common substring then is from index end – res + 1 to index end in s1.

Following is the pseudocode of our approach:

```
dp[][] = 2D array N x M
result = 0, r = 0, c = 0

for i from 0 to M + 1
   for j from 0 to N + 1
      if (i == 0 or j == 0)
         dp[i][j] = 0
      else if (S1[i-1] == S2[j-1])
         dp[i][j] = dp[i-1][j-1] + 1
         if (result < dp[i][j])
         {
            result = dp[i][j];
            r = i;
            c = j;
         }
      else
         dp[i][j] = 0

result is our answer
```

The basic condition of calculating dp[][] is result of current row in matrix dp[][] depends on values from previous row. Hence the required length of longest common substring can be **obtained by maintaining values of two consecutive rows only**, thereby reducing space requirements to **O(2 * N)**.

This would result in the following pseudocode:

```
dp[][] = 2D array 2 x M
result = 0, r = 0, c = 0
current = 0

for i from 0 to M + 1
  for j from 0 to N + 1
    if (i == 0 or j == 0)
      dp[current][j] = 0
    else if (S1[i-1] == S2[j-1])
      dp[current][j] = dp[current-1][j-1] + 1
      if (result < dp[current][j])
      {
        result = dp[current][j];
        r = i;
        c = j;
      }
    else
      dp[current][j] = 0
    current = 1 - current

result is our answer
```

Example

For instance, if we consider string doll as str1 and another string dog as str2 and loop through all characters of str1,position denoted by i, and str2,position denoted by j, to build the table dp[][].

We consider the variable curr to state the current row which toggles its value to 0 and 1 at the end of every outer iteration.

When i=0 we all the values of dp[][] corresponding to the first row is set 0.When i=1 and str1[i-1]!=str2[j-1], dp[curr][j] = 0.

When str1[i-1] = str2[j-1] = 'd' (at j=1) , dp[cur][j] = dp[1][1] = dp[1-curr][j-1] + 1 = 0+1 =1. We store the maximum length of longest common substring (maximum value of dp[cur][j]) as res and the ending index of the substring as end. Here res=1 and end=0.

When i=2 and j=2, curr=0, str1[i-1] = 'o' and str2[j-1] = 'o'.Since str1[i-1] = str2[j-1] therefore dp[curr][j] = dp[1-curr][j-1] + 1 = dp[1][1] + 1 = 1 + 1 = 2.

Since res = 1 which is less than dp[curr][j], res = dp[curr][j] = 2 and end = i-1 = 1.

All other positions of dp is less than res. So, finally the length of the largest common substring between doll and dog is 2.

To retrieve the substring iterate from position end-res+1 i.e. 1-2+1 = 0 till end i.e. 1 in str1 doll to get do as the largest common substring between dog and doll.

Since we are using two for loops for both the strings ,therefore the time complexity of finding the longest common substring using dynamic programming approach is **O(N * M)** where n and m are the lengths of the strings. Since this implementation involves only two rows and n columns for building dp[][],therefore, the space complexity would be **O(2 * N)**.

Hence, this problem demonstrates the strength of Dynamic Programming approach. Following is the summary of the approaches:

- Brute force **O(N⁴) time, O(1) space**
- Hashing approach **O(N²) time, O(N²) space**
- Dynamic Programming **O(N²) time, O(N) space**

Think of the approaches deeply as it gives deep insights on the link of Dynamic Programming and Hashing techniques.

We just solved an important Dynamic Programming approach for string-based problems

---

Problem 3: XOR value

Given an array of size N and a value M, we must find the number of subsets in the array having M as the XOR value of all elements in the subset. XOR gives 1 as output when there are odd number of 1s in the input or else, it will give 0 as output.

Example of XOR:

- 1 xor 0 xor 1 = 0
- 1 xor 0 = 1
- 0 xor 0 = 0

XOR of a binary number is computed by taking XOR of each corresponding digit like

$$1101101$$

$$0010011$$

$$1010101$$

$$XOR = 0101011$$

Example of our problem:

Input: arr[] = {1, 2, 3, 4}, M = 4

Output: 2 (there are 2 such subsets)

The subsets having XOR value as 4 are:

```
{4}, {1, 2, 3, 4}
```

As

- 4 = 4
- 1 xor 2 xor 3 xor 4 = 001 xor 010 xor 011 xor 100 = 100

Other subsets that do not satisfy the condition are:

```
{3, 4}, {1, 2, 4} and many more
```

We have explored two approaches to solve this problem:

- Brute force approach **O(2^N) time, O(1) space**
- Dynamic Programming **O(N * K) time, O(N * K) space**

As you should have realized, this is a unique problem as Dynamic Programming solves the problem extremely efficiently compared to the brute force approach as the search space is of exponential size but we are finding the global maxima in linear time.

Brute force approach

The brute force approach is to generate all subsets and count subsets for which XOR of all elements is equal to a given number.

Steps:

- Set count A to 0
- For each subset S1 of set S

- Calculate XOR of all elements of subset S1
- If XOR is equal to A, then increment count A

For a given set of N elements, there are 2^N subsets as each element can be included or removed from a subset.

For a given set of N elements, finding the XOR of all elements will take $O(N)$ time and hence, the overall time complexity of this brute force approach will be $O(N \times 2^N)$ with a space complexity of $O(1)$ if we do not store all subsets at once.

Generating all 2^N subsequences are be challenging but the basic idea is to use the binary representation of integers to determine which element to include. For example, the representation 001011 shows a subset where 1st, 2nd and 4th elements (1s) are included.

For a set of N elements, we need to use integers from **0 to 2^N-1**.

This is a simple yet one of the most powerful implementation techniques.

We covered this point of subsequence generation in detail in our book:

Problems for the day before your coding interview by Aditya Chatterjee & Ue Kiao (OpenGenus).

Problems for the day before your coding interview

By Aditya Chatterjee & Ue Kiao

OpenGenus.org

Get the book now: **daybefore1.opengenus.org**

At this point, it is clear that:

- There are an exponential number of possibilities $O(2^N)$
- We need to avoid checking all possibilities
- We need to utilize some property of XOR

Dynamic Programming

We will use Dynamic programming approach to solve this problem efficiently.

In the table DP[i][j] signifies number of subsets with XOR j till the elements from 1st to i^{th} are taken into consideration.

```
DP[i][j] = number of subsets with XOR 'j' till the elements
from 1st to ith element
```

If we are at i^{th} element of the array and traverse the row for the $(i-1)^{th}$ element we get the subsets number of subsets of all possible XOR values.

For the ith element if we get DP[i-1][j]>0, it means that XOR value j-1 has that many number of subsets.

Hence, we take XOR of arr[i] with this value and get the resulting number of subsets of the new XOR value (say x) by adding:

- the previous number of subsets of x which will be given by DP[i-1][((j-1)^arr[i-2])+1]
- number of subsets with XOR value j-1 which is equal to DP[i-1][j]

Relation:

$$DP[i][((j-1) \wedge arr[i-2]) + 1] = DP[i-1][((j-1) \wedge arr[i-2]) + 1] + DP[i-1][j]$$

For generating the values in DP table we take DP[1][1]=1 which represents there is always a null subset having XOR value 0. This will be the base case for the approach used.

Implementation approach

The maximum possible XOR value of any subset will be pow(2,((log2(max(arr))+1))) − 1. Let this number be equal to k.

Hence, we take the number of columns of the 2-D array to be k+2 and number of rows to be N+2. Now we define the array as DP[N+2][k+2].

For the given example:

```
arr[]={1,2,3,4}
k=pow(2,log2(4)+1)-1=7
```

As the maximum XOR value will be 7, so there will be 5 rows (4 elements + 1 to denote no element) and 8 columns (0 to 7). Our Dynamic Programming table will look like this:

	-1	0	1	2	3	4	5	6	7
-1	1	0	0	0	0	0	0	0
1	.	.	.	.	.	.	.	.
2	.	.	.	.	.	.	.	.
3	.	.	.	.	.	.	.	.
4	.	.	.	.	.	.	.	.

Note that elements in the first column and first row are just placeholders to denote the corresponding XOR value and input element. In actual implementation, it may not be stored.

We set DP[1][1]=1 as there is always a subset i.e. (null set) which has XOR value=0.

Now start traversing the array from i=2 and for each DP[i][j] we check if DP[i-1][j]>0 we go to element DP[i][j^arr[i-2]+1) and increase it's value by DP[i-1][j]+DP[i-1][j^arr[i-2]+1] as now the subset count of j^arr[i-2] will increase by the number of subsets having XOR value as j.

Step by step example:

We traverse the given array and update the values in the DP table accordingly.

As arr[0]=1 so we check which subset value in the above row has frequency>0 here it is 0 so we update the value of DP[2][0^1+1] by DP[1][1]+DP[1][2].

Follow the relation to calculate the values manually and verify it.

-1	0	1	2	3	4	5	6	7
-1	1	0	0	0	0	0	0	0
1	1	1	0	0	0	0	0	0
2	.	.	.	.	.	.	.	.
3	.	.	.	.	.	.	.	.
4	.	.	.	.	.	.	.	.

Likewise we do it for **arr[1]=2**.

Follow the relation to calculate the values manually and verify it.

-1	0	1	2	3	4	5	6	7
-1	1	0	0	0	0	0	0	0
1	1	1	0	0	0	0	0	0
2	1	1	1	1	0	0	0	0
3	.	.	.	.	.	.	.	.
4	.	.	.	.	.	.	.	.

Likewise for **arr[2]=3**

Follow the relation to calculate the values manually and verify it.

-1	0	1	2	3	4	5	6	7
-1	1	0	0	0	0	0	0	0
1	1	1	0	0	0	0	0	0
2	1	1	1	1	0	0	0	0
3	2	2	2	2	0	0	0	0
4	.	.	.	.	.	.	.	.

Likewise for **arr[3]=4**

Follow the relation to calculate the values manually and verify it.

	-1	0	1	2	3	4	5	6	7
-1	1	0	0	0	0	0	0	0
1	1	1	0	0	0	0	0	0
2	1	1	1	1	0	0	0	0
3	2	2	2	2	0	0	0	0
4	2	2	2	2	2	2	2	2

Following is the pseudocode of our Dynamic Programming approach:

```
input[]  // array
M  // Given XOR value
L = length(input)

//Calculating the maximum possible xor value
max_xor = 0
for(i=0; i < L; i++)
{
    max_xor = MAXIMUM(max_xor, input[i]);
}

int K = (1 << (int)(log2(max_xor) + 1) ) - 1;

DP[L+2][K+2]

// Base cases
DP[0][0]=-1;
DP[1][0]=-1;

//filling all possible xor values in the first row
for(i=1; i < K+2; i++)
{
    DP[0][i]=i-1;
    DP[1][i]=0;
}

//filling all the array elements in the first column
for(i=2; i < L+2; i++)
```

```
{
    DP[i][0]=arr[i-2];
}

DP[1][1]=1;
//Filling the DP table as per relation
for(i=2; i < L+2; i++)
{
    for(j=1;j < K+2;j++)
    {
        if(DP[i-1][j]!=0)
        {
            DP[i][((j-1)^arr[i-2])+1] =
                DP[i-1][((j-1)^arr[i-2])+1]+DP[i-1][j];
        }
    }
    for(j=1; j < K+2; j++)
    {
        DP[i][j]=max(DP[i-1][j],DP[i][j]);
    }
}

DP[L+1][M+1] is our answer
```

Complexity

The time complexity of the given approach is **O(K * N)** where

- K is the maximum possible XOR value
- N is the total number of elements in the array

The space complexity of our approach is **O(N * K)** as well.

Hence, following is the summary of the two approaches we have explored:

- Brute force approach **O(2^N) time, O(1) space**

- Dynamic Programming **O(N * K) time, O(N * K) space**

We just solved a Mathematical problem using Dynamic Programming and found global maxima in an exponential search space

---

Problem 4: K edge Path

We will, now, investigate a graph-based problem where a Dynamic Programming approach is a relatively efficient approach, but a better approach exists. Usually, in interviews, difficult problems can be modeled as a graph-based problem following which it is easy to solve.

This problem is special as:

- It shows how native approaches like Dynamic Programming can be applied to a graph problem
- It presents a case where a divide and conquer approach is faster than a Dynamic Programming approach
- It illustrates key ideas which can be used to solve one of the toughest graph problems

The problem is that given a graph, we need to find the number of paths from a vertex (say u) to another vertex (say v) with exactly K edges. Let us define that the graph has V vertices and E edges.

Pause and think for a couple of minutes before proceeding further.

This might seem to be a simple problem but solving this efficiently will require great insights. We will solve this step by step and go through three approaches:

- **Brute force** O(V^K) time

- **Dynamic Programming** O(V^3 * K) time

- **Divide and Conquer** O(V^3 * logK) time

Let us start with the brute force approach. This is a simple approach as we just need to traverse the graph and keep track of the edges encountered. A simple way is to implement it recursively.

The recursive structure will be as:

paths (adjacency_matrix, source_vertex, destination_vertex, edges_permitted)

We start with the source vertex as u and then, move to all adjacent vertices of u and make a recursive call on that vertex as the source vertex. In this case, the edges permitted is decremented by 1 as we have already traversed an edge.

We add up all recursive calls which successfully reach the destination vertex using all the edges as permitted. If is simple to manage as if destination vertex is reach and edges permitted goes to 0, we have found a path and we return 1. In other cases, we shall return 0. We will add up all such return values and get our answer.

The pseudocode is as follows:

```
int numberOfPathsNaive(2D array adj, int u, int v, int k)
{
    int __v = adj.size();
    if(k == 0 && u == v)
        return 1;
    if(k == 1 && adj[u][v])
        return 1;
    if(k <= 0)
        return 0;
    int res = 0;
    for(int i = 0; i < __v; ++ i)
    {
        if(adj[u][i])
        {
            res += numberOfPathsNaive(adj, i, v, k - 1);
        }
    }
    return res;
}
```

As we are traversing the entire graph with all possible edges, the time complexity of our brute force approach is exponential that is $O(V^K)$ where V is the number of vertices and K is the number of edges.

As a path can have at most K edges (without loops) and each edge can have any of the V vertices as pairs, the total number of possible paths becomes $O(V^K)$ from which we need to find the number of paths that is within our focus.

As our brute force approach takes exponential time, it is not practical to use it for graphs beyond a certain size. We need to find an optimal approach.

We will take up a **Dynamic Programming approach** to solve this problem which will give a major boost.

In dynamic programing approach we use a 3D matrix table to store the number of paths, **dp[i][j][e]** stores the number of paths from i to j with exactly e edges.

We fill the table in bottom up manner, we start from e=0 and fill the table till e=k. Then we have our answer stored in dp[u][v][k] where u is source, v is destination and k is number edges between path from source to destination.

dp[u][v][k] = number of paths from u to v with k edges

The idea of the relation is if there is an edge between vertex i and b, then dp[i][j][e] += dp[b][j][e-1] as one edge has been covered while going from vertex i to b.

The number of paths from vertex b to j is included in the set of paths from vertex i to j because there is an edge from vertex i to b.

Following code snippet covers the idea:

```
for(int b = 0; b < __v ; ++b)
    if(adj[i][b])
        dp[i][j][e] += dp[b][j][e - 1];
```

The pseudocode is as follows:

```
for(int e = 0; e <= k; ++ e)
{
    for(int i = 0;i < __v; ++ i)
    {
        for(int j = 0;j < __v; ++ j)
        {
            // initialize
            dp[i][j][e] = 0;

            // base cases
            if(e == 0 && i == j)
                dp[i][j][e] = 1;
            if(e == 1 && adj[i][j])
                dp[i][j][e] = 1;

            // go to adjacent edges only when number of edges is more
than 1
            if(e>1)
            {
                for(int b = 0; b < __v ; ++ b)
```

```
        {
            if(adj[i][b])
            {
                dp[i][j][e] += dp[b][j][e - 1];
            }
        }
    }
  }
}
// number of paths from u to v with k edges
return dp[u][v][k];
```

If you observe carefully, the time complexity to calculate dp[u][v][k] is $O(V^3 * K)$. We have improved this significantly as we have gone from an exponential time complexity to a polynomial time complexity.

We can optimize this further by using a **divide and conquer approach**.

We can use divide and conquer approach to solve this problem in $O(V^3 \log_2 k)$ time, to this we use the fact that the number of paths of length k from u to v is the [u][v]th entry in the matrix $(adj[V][V])^k$.

The kth power of a graph G is a graph with the same set of vertices as G and an edge between two vertices if and only if there is a path of length at most k between them. Since a path of length two between vertices u and v exists for every vertex w such that {u,w} and {w,v} are edges in G, the square of the adjacency matrix of G counts the number of such paths. Similarly, the [u][v]th element of the kth power of the adjacency matrix of G gives the number of paths of length k between vertices u and v.

To understand why this holds true, follow along. In the first case of adjacency matrix, it is natural that it holds true as a path of length 1 is one edge which is that the two vertices are directly connected.

When we raised the adjacency matrix to the power of 2, for a given index, we compute the multiplication of that particular row with the column that passes through the index. Let the index be (x, y). In this case, the row denotes how vertex x is connected to other vertices. The column denotes how other vertices are connected to vertex y.

When we are multiplying this, we are computing the combination of elements of a row with elements of the column. In our case, a row represents how a vertex is linked to other vertices and the column represents how other vertices are linked with the current vertex. By multiplying, we are incrementally increasing the length of path.

This is an important concept. Think about this deeply.

At this point, if we simply perform multiplication and get the adjacency matrix raised to the power of K, we will get the same time complexity.

To improve it, we need to optimize this step which can be done using the idea that raising to the power of 2 eliminates several multiplications.

For example, instead of computing power of 5, we can compute 2 times power of 2 followed by a multiplication which results in the same answer.

To find $(adj[V][V])^k$, we use the divide and conquer approach of finding power(x, y) in $O(log_2 y)$ time that is this algorithm is an application of **fast matrix exponentiation**.

Fast matrix exponentiation is based on the same principle we explained and is applicable on numeric data other than matrix as well.

The idea is:

$$A^N = (A^{N/2})^2 \text{ if N is even}$$

$$A^N = (A^{(N-1)/2})^2 * A \text{ if N is odd}$$

This is computed recursively that is same rules apply to $A^{N/2}$ as to A^N. This reduces the number of multiplications from N to logN.

The pseudocode of this approach is as follows:

```
// Function to compute adjacency_matrix raise to power k.
```

```
power(adjacency_matrix, u, v, k)
{
    __v = adj.size();
    result[][];

    for(int i = 0; i < __v; ++i)
        result [i][i] = 1;

    while (k > 0)
    {
        if (k % 2 == 1)
            result = multiply(result, adjacency_matrix);
        adjacency_matrix = multiply(adjacency_matrix,
adjacency_matrix);
        k /= 2;
    }
    // number of paths from u to v with k edges
    return result [u][v];
}
```

Following is the complexity summary of the approaches we have explored:

Time Complexity

- Brute force approach takes $O(V^k)$ time.

- DP approach takes $O(V^3 k)$ time.

- Divide and Conquer approach takes $O(V^3 \log_2 k)$ time.

Space Complexity

- Brute force approach takes $O(V^2)$ auxiliary space and $O(V^k)$ stack space.

- DP approach takes $O(V^2k)$ auxiliary space.

- Divide and conquer takes $O(V^2)$ auxiliary space.

Hence, we can see that our final divide and conquer approach works better than the Dynamic Programming approach both in terms of time and space complexity.

We just solved a problem that is in the intersection of Graph Theory and Dynamic Programming. Enjoy.

With this problem, we have come to the end of the short guide on Dynamic Programming. Think about the above problems deeply as it captures several insights which will enable you to solve problems using approaches other than Dynamic Programming as well.

CONCLUDING NOTE

As a next step, you may randomly pick a problem from this book, read the problem statement and dive into designing your own solution and implement it in a Programming Language of your choice.

Remember, we are here to help you. If you have any doubts in a problem, you can contact us (team@opengenus.org) anytime.

Dynamic Programming is a powerful Algorithmic technique which can help you tackle complex problems easily.

Now on completing this book, you have conquered this core domain of Algorithm.

For more practice and contribute to Computing Community, feel free to join our Internship Program:

internship.OPENGENUS.org.

BE A NATIONAL PROGRAMMER

www.ingramcontent.com/pod-product-compliance
Lightning Source LLC
Chambersburg PA
CBHW080544060326
40690CB00022B/5214